REFLECTIONS

Compiled by Michael Ryan
Cover Design by Bridgewater Design Consultants

Great Quotations Publishing Company

Published in the United States by Great Quotations Publishing Co., 1967 Quincy Ct., Glendale Heights, IL 60139

Printed in Hong Kong.

ISBN 1-56245-033-6

For Isabel

Too often we get caught up in the daily activities of life and lose touch with what is truly important. Personal experience has taught us that centering ourselves in the face of life's demands smooths our passages. This book is dedicated to those of you who seek a life of greater inner peace and inspiration. We've gathered these quotations from men and women of many lands and times, to let them stimulate our own reflections. The words remind us that everyone has pondered, struggled and succeeded, in much the same way as we. They are all like us. We are all like them. We hope that these thoughts will inspire you. Enjoy.

The universe is transformation; our life is what our thoughts make it.

Marcus Aurelius Antoninus

4

Remember, one thought does not mean much. But thoughts that we think over and over are like drops of water: at first there are just a few; and then after awhile you've created a pool... then a lake... and then an ocean.

It may be those who do most,
dream most.

Stephen Leacock

The distance doesn't matter;
only the first step is difficult.

Mme. du Deffand

I have learned silence from the talkative; tolerance from the intolerant and kindness from the unkind. I should not be ungrateful to those teachers.

Kahlil Gibran

8

Hope is a good breakfast,
but it is a bad supper.

Francis Bacon

There's a period of life when we swallow a knowledge of ourselves and it becomes either good or sour inside.

Pearl Bailey

10

If we try too hard to force others to live in our world, because we think it is the real world, we are doomed to disappointment.

William Glasser, M.D.

There is nothing so moving – not even acts of love or hate – as the discovery that one is not alone.

Robert Ardrey

We are whole beings.
We know this somewhere in a part of ourselves that feels like memory.

Susan Griffin

I take it to be a principle of life, not to be too much addicted to any one thing.

Terence

Try to keep the rebel artist alive in you, no matter how attractive or exhausting the temptation.

Norman Mailer

It is not what we see and touch or that which others do for us which makes us happy; it is that which we think and feel and do, first for the other fellow and then for ourselves.

Helen Keller

Any path is only a path, and there is no affront, to oneself or to others, in dropping if that is what your heart tells you.

Carlos Castaneda

Within our dreams and aspirations we find opportunities.

Sue Atchley Ebaugh

There are two tragedies in life. One is not to get your heart's desire. The other is to get it.

George Bernard Shaw

I like to listen.
I have learned a great deal from listening carefully. Most people never listen.

Ernest Hemingway

A belief which does not spring from a conviction in the emotions is no belief at all.

Evelyn Scott

Dreams are… illustrations from the book your soul is writing about you.

Marsha Norman

I've arrived at this outermost edge of my life by my own actions. Where I am is thoroughly unacceptable. Therefore, I must stop doing what I've been doing.

Alice Koller

If you would be loved, love and be lovable.

Benjamin Franklin

If you can imagine it, you can achieve it. If you can dream it, you can become it.

William Arthur Ward

26

P aradoxical as it may seem, to believe in youth is to look backward; to look forward we must believe in age.

Dorothy L. Sayers

I have a right to my anger, and I don't want anybody telling me I shouldn't be, that it's not nice to be, and that something's wrong with me because I get angry.

28

One has to have a bit of neurosis to go on being an artist. A balanced human seldom produces art. It's that imbalance which impels us.

Beverly Pepper

The beauty of the world...
has two edges, one of laughter,
one of anguish, cutting the heart
asunder.

Virginia Woolf

Over the years our bodies become walking autobiographies, telling friends and strangers alike of the minor and major stresses of our lives.

Marilyn Ferguson

Life comes in clusters, clusters of solitude, then a cluster when there is hardly time to breathe.

May Sarton

I nside myself is a place where I live all alone and that's where you renew your springs that never dry up.

Pearl S. Buck

If one is going to change things, one has to make a fuss and catch the eye of the world.

Elizabeth Janeway

We will be victorious if we have not forgotten to learn.

Rosa Luxemburg

To keep your character intact, you cannot stoop to filthy acts. It makes it easier to stoop the next time.

Katherine Hepburn

However much we guard against it, we tend to shape ourselves in the image others have of us.

Eric Hoffer

All I have seen teaches me to trust the creator for all I have not seen.

Ralph Waldo Emerson

Better keep yourself clean and bright; you are the window through which you must see the world.

George Bernard Shaw

All humans are frightened of their own solitude. Yet only in solitude can we learn to know ourselves, learn to handle our own eternity of aloneness.

Han Suyin

To expect life to be tailored to our specifications is to invite frustration.

Unknown

The solution to my life occurred to me one evening while I was ironing a shirt.

Alice Munro

Happiness is a byproduct of an effort to make somebody else happy.

Gretta Brooker Palmer

I don't wait for moods. You accomplish nothing if you do that. Your mind must know it has got to get down to earth.

Pearl S. Buck

One cannot collect all the beautiful shells on the beach, one can collect only a few.

Anne Morrow Lindbergh

One often learns more from ten days of agony than from ten years of contentment.

Merle Shain

I am ashamed of these tears. And yet at the extreme of my misfortune I am ashamed not to shed them.

Euripides

Noble deeds and hot baths are the best cures for depression.

Dodie Smith

There are two ways of spreading light: to be the candle or the mirror that reflects it.

Edith Wharton

Some things... arrive on their own mysterious hour, on their own terms and not yours, to be seized or relinquished forever.

Gail Godwin

W̲e don't see things as they are,
we see them as we are.

Anais Nin

If you shut your door to all errors, truth will be shut out.

Rabindranath Tagore

Relationships are only alive as the people engaging in them.

Donald B. Ardell

To live in dialogue with another is to live twice. Joys are doubled by exchange and burdens are cut in half.

Wishart

I think I must let go. Must fear not, must be quiet so that my children can hear the Sound of Creation and dance the dance that is in them.

Russel Hoban

The game of life is a game of boomerangs. Our thoughts, deeds, and words return to us sooner or later, with astounding accuracy.

Florence Scovel Shinn

I search in these words and find
nothing more than myself,
caught between the grapes and the
thorns.

Anne Sexton

S peak your truth quietly and clearly; and listen to others, even to the dull and the ignorant; they too have their story.

Max Ehrmann

You must not change one thing,
one pebble, one grain of sand,
until you know what good and evil
will follow that act.

Ursula K. LeGuin

Kill the snake of doubt in your soul, crush the worms of fear in your heart and mountains will move out of your way.

Kate Seredy

Each friend represents a world in us, a world possibly not born until they arrive, and it is only by this meeting that a new world is born.

Anais Nin

I always felt that the great high privilege, relief and comfort of friendship was that one had to explain nothing.

Katherine Mansfield

Nobody has ever measured,
even poets, how much a heart
can hold.

Zelda Fitzgerald

I came into this world, not chiefly to make this a good place to live in, but to live in it, be it good or bad.

H. D. Thoreau

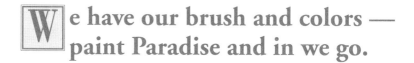

We have our brush and colors —
paint Paradise and in we go.

Nikos Kazantzakis

Imagination has always had the powers of resurrection that no science can match.

Ingrid Bengis

To be happy means to be free,
not from pain or fear, but from
care or anxiety.

W.H. Auden

Every worthwhile accomplishment, big or little, has its stages of drudgery and triumph; a beginning, a struggle, and a victory.

Anonymous

Eternity is called whole, not because it has parts, but because it is lacking in nothing.

Thomas Aquinas

Thoughts held in mind produce their kind.

Anonymous

All great reforms require one to dare a lot to win a little.

William L. O'Neill

Happiness is not a matter of events; it depends upon the tides of the mind.

Alice Meynell

M y life is increasingly an inner one and the outer setting matters less and less.

Etty Hillesum

Mistakes are part of the dues
one pays for a full life.

Sophia Loren

We can do no great things —
only small things with great love.

Mother Teresa

78

Life is what happens to us while we are making other plans.

Thomas La Mance

One word frees us of all the weight and pain of life. That word is love.

Sophocles
(c. 495-406 B.C.)

Our aspirations are our possibilities.

Robert Browning

I magine there's no country. It isn't hard to do. Nothing to kill or die for. And no religion, too.

John Lennon

I dream my painting, and then I paint my dreams.

Vincent Van Gogh

84

Art is the only way to run away without leaving home.

Twyla Tharp

Look for a long time at what pleases you, and for a longer time at what pains you.

Colette

Let the world know you as you are, not as you think you should be, because sooner or later, if you are posing, you will forget the pose, and then where are you?

Fanny Brice

The more abstract the truth you want to teach, the more thoroughly you must seduce the senses to accept it.

Freidrich Nietzsche

A true friend is the most precious of all possessions and the one we take the least thought about acquiring.

La Rochefoucauld
(1613-1680)

The best and the most beautiful things in the world cannot be seen, nor touched... but are felt in the heart.

Helen Keller

All our resolves and decisions are made in a mood or frame of mind which is certain to change.

Marcel Proust

L ife is a battle in which we fall from wounds we recieve in running away.

William L. Sullivan

When you hold resentment toward another, you are bound to that person or condition by an emotional link that is stronger than steel.

Catherine Ponder

It is better to deserve honors and not have them than to have them and not deserve them.

Mark Twain

L ove is the immortal flow of energy that nourishes, extends and preserves. Its eternal goal is life.

Smiley Blanton

We are all born for love. It is the principle of exsistence, and its only end.

Benjamin Disraeli

When you cease to dream,
you cease to live.

Malcolm S. Forbes

Cherish your visions and your dreams as they are the children of your soul; the blueprints of your ultimate achievements.

Napoleon Hill

Love is everything. It is the key to life, and its influences are those that move the world.

Ralph Waldo Trine

You take people as far as they will go, not as far as you would like them to go.

Jeannette Rankin

There are some things you learn best in calm, and some in storm.

Willa Cather

I am imagination. I can see what the eyes cannot see. I can hear what the ears cannot hear. I can feel what the heart cannot feel.

Peter Nivio Zarlenga

L ife is like a great jazz riff. You sense the end the very moment you were wanting it to go on forever.

Sheila Ballantyne

Life without love is like a tree without blossom and fruit.

Kahlil Gibran

Life offstage has sometimes been a wilderness of unpredictables in an unchoreographed world.

Margot Fonteyn

The more sand that has escaped from the hourglass of our life, the clearer we should see through it.

Jean Paul

Once you have learned to love,
you will have learned to live.

Don't compromise yourself.
You are all you've got.

Betty Ford

I don't want to live —
I want to love first,
and live incidentally.

Zelda Fitzgerald

L ove opens the doors into everything, as far as I can see, including and perhaps most of all, the door into one's own secret, and often terrible and frightening, real self.

Do you know the hallmark of the second-rater? It's resentment of another man's achievement.

112

I can sometimes resist temptation, but never mischief.

Joyce Rebeta-Burditt

Those who bring sunshine to the lives of others cannot keep it from themselves.

James Barrie

The moment you have in your heart this extraordinary thing called love and feel the depth, the delight, the ecstasy of it, you will discover that for you the world is transformed.

Music has been my playmate, my lover, and my crying towel.

Buffy Sainte-Marie

Nothing contributes so much to tranquilize the mind as a steady purpose — a point on which the soul may fix its intellectual eye.

Mary Shelley

When one's own problems are unsolvable and all best efforts frustated, it is lifesaving to listen to other people's problems.

Suzanne Massie

When a man comes to me for advice, I find out the kind of advice he wants, and I give it to him.

Josh Billings

When a great poet has lived, certain things have been done once for all, and cannot be achieved again.

T.S. Eliot

Mystic: a person who is puzzled before the obvious, but who understands the non-existent.

S ecrets are rarely betrayed or discovered according to any program our fear has sketched out.

George Eliot

We live on the leash of our senses.

Diane Ackerman

Service is the rent you pay for room on this earth.

Shirley Chisholm

You mustn't force sex to do the work of love or love to do the work of sex — that's quite a thought, isn't it?

Mary McCarthy

T he great pleasure in life is doing what people say you cannot do.

Walter Bagehot

If there were any justice in the world, people would be able to fly over pigeons for a change.

Anonymous

Dreams say what they mean, but they don't say it in a daytime language.

Gail Godwin

It is while trying to get everything straight in my head that I get confused.

Mary Virginia Micka

I postpone death by living, by suffering, by error, by risking, by giving, by losing.

Anais Nin

The strongest principle of growth lies in the human choice.

George Eliot

People change and forget to tell each other.

Lillian Hellman

The limits of my language
mean the limits of my world.

Ludwig Wittgenstein

To jealousy, nothing is more frightful than laughter.

Francoise Sagan

Nature never repeats herself, and the possibilities of one human soul will never be found in another.

Elizabeth Cady Stanton

I have met with women who I really think would like to be married to a poem, and to be given away by a novel.

John Keats

Make voyages. Attempt them.
There's nothing else.

Tennessee Williams

It is characteristic of wisdom not to do desperate things.

Henry David Thoreau

The truth is cruel, but it can be loved, and it makes free those who have loved it.

George Santayana

141

Truth is something you stumble into when you think you're going some place else.

Jerry Garcia

142

It is the function of vice to keep virtue within reasonable grounds.

Samuel Butler

The Saints are Sinners who keep on trying.

Robert Louis Stevenson

This world is not conclusion.
A sequel stands beyond;
invisible as music, but positive
as sound.

Emily Dickinson

I love my past. I love my present. I'm not ashamed of what I've had, and I'm not sad because I have it no longer.

Colette

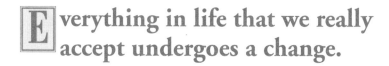 **E**verything in life that we really accept undergoes a change.

Katherine Mansfield

I can't think of any sorrow in the world that a hot bath wouldn't help, just a little bit.

Susan Glaspell

I have never seen a greater monster or miracle in the world than myself.

Montaigne

150

W̄e judge ourselves by our motives and others by their actions.

Dwight Morrow

Be yourself. Who else is better qualified?

Frank J. Giblin, II

C ompassion for myself is the
most powerful healer of
them all.

Theodore Isaac Rubin

I am more afraid of my own heart than of the Pope and all his cardinals. I have within me the great Pope, Self.

Martin Luther

There are limits to self-indulgence, none to self-restraint.

Gandhi

My great mistake, the fault for which I can't forgive myself, is that one day I ceased my obstinate pursuit of my own individuality.

Oscar Wilde

If we go down into ourselves we find that we possess exactly what we desire.

Simone Weil

The tragedy of life is that people do not change.

Agatha Christie

C haracter builds slowly,
but it can be torn down with
incredible swiftness.

Faith Baldwin

P eople have to learn sometimes
not only how much the heart,
but how much the head, can bear.

Maria Mitchell

160

I am one of those who never knows the direction of my journey until I have almost arrived.

Anna Louise Strong

I am never afraid of
what I know.

Anna Sewell

162

It is in his pleasure that a man really lives; it is from his leisure that he constructs the true fabric of self.

Agnes Repplier

164

Without friends no one would choose to live, though he had all other goods.

Aristotle

God is a comedian whose
audience is afraid to laugh.

H.L. Mencken

Happiness is essentially a state of going somewhere, wholeheartedly, one-directionally, without regret or reservation.

William H. Sheldon

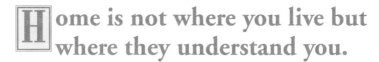 **ome is not where you live but where they understand you.**

Christian Morgenstern